Horse Therapists

Judith Janda Presnall

KidHaven Press, an imprint of Gale Group, Inc.
10911 Technology Place, San Diego, CA 92127

Dedication

To all those involved with horse therapy:
Your caring service to children with disabilities
and kindness to the horses is touching.

Acknowledgments

The author wishes to express her gratitude to these four women who reviewed the manuscript and donated their time and efforts in the creation of this book: Connie M. Gilly, director, Special Equestrian Riding Therapy (SERT); Therapeutic Riding Center, Chatsworth, California; Gloria Hamblin, director, Ride on Therapeutic Horsemanship, Chatsworth, California; Liz Helms, director, Ahead with Horses, Inc., Sun Valley, California; Nancy Pitchford, director, Heads Up, Inc., Saugus, California.

Library of Congress Cataloging-in-Publication Data
Presnall, Judith Janda.
    Horse therapists / by Judith Janda Presnall.
       p. cm. — (Animals with jobs)
    Includes bibliographical references and index
    Summary: Discusses the use of horseback riding as therapy for the physically and emotionally disabled.
    ISBN 0–7377–0615–5 (hardback alk. paper)
    1. Horsemanship—Therapeutic use—Juvenile literature.
    [1. Horsemanship—Therapeutic use. 2. Horses.] I. Title. II. Series.

    RM931.H6 P74 2002
    615.8'515—dc21

    00–012807

Contents

Introduction

The Horse's Natural Gift

People have been riding horses for centuries for pleasure and transportation. But many people do not realize that horses are also used to help the handicapped. Through use in a special type of therapy, horses offer emotional and physical help to children and adults with **disabilities**.

The natural motion of the horse gently exercises the rider's spinal column, pelvis, muscles, and joints. The rider's body moves up and down, sways side to side, and rocks back and forth. The movement for a rider is similar to the human walk. The horse's movements seem to unlock an instinctual response from the rider—relaxing tight muscles and toning weak ones.

For the physically disabled, the goals of horse therapy may include strengthening muscles, developing balance and coordination, and even the long-term goal of walking. For an emotionally disabled person, the goal may be learning to speak or to gain confidence, patience, and self-esteem. This happens when the rider begins to bond with the horse and relate to people around him or her.

In horse therapy, a trained horse, an instructor or **therapist**, and volunteers work together to reach the rider's goals. This may take the rider months or years to achieve, but each success, no matter how small, creates happiness and pride for everyone involved. And the horse is a partner all along the way.

Horse therapy benefits people with disabilities and illnesses such as **cerebral palsy**, **spina bifida**, and **multiple sclerosis**. All are conditions that affect the body's

Horseback riding benefits people with many different kinds of disabilities.

A padded saddle allows riders close contact with the horse.

muscles, nerves, and spine. People born with **Down's syndrome**, **mental retardation**, and **autism**, in which the brain is affected, can also improve.

Nine-year-old Josh is among those who have experienced horseback riding therapy. Josh was born with cerebral palsy, a condition that results from damage to the motor areas of the brain, either before, during, or after birth.

Josh cannot walk or stand without the help of leg braces and a walker. He cannot sit without support. He cannot hold his head steady. But when Josh sits astride a moving horse, his muscles become active and his arms and legs feel a flow of energy and firmness. He sits taller and straighter in the saddle than he can in a chair. To allow as much body-to-body contact as possible, the animal wears a soft pad saddle. The warmth of the horse aids in relaxing Josh's legs. His head does not wobble. The horse's **gait** makes this possible. Horses **walk** with a rhythmic and repetitive gait.

This activity has proved helpful to Josh, whose muscles are weak. After five years of horseback riding therapy, Josh no longer needs his leg braces. He moves around using only his walker.

The muscles of the back, stomach, and arms become stronger from horseback riding therapy.

Horses are smart animals who often seem to grasp the importance of their jobs. "The horses seem to understand they are carrying very special burdens," a director says. "Put our riders on their backs and even spirited animals become the gentlest creatures. They *know*."[1]

One father describes his seven-year-old daughter Sammi Jo, who has cerebral palsy, and her reaction to horse therapy. "As soon as we pull up to the hospital for her weekly session, she starts crying," he says. "But here, [at the therapy ranch] she's happy. Look!"[2] The father gestures toward a giggling little girl poised atop a mare named Lilly.

Chapter One

Horse Training

The success of any riding program depends on many factors, but the most important element is the horse. The selection of horses depends on several requirements including temperament, age, size, gait, and sex.

Above all else, horses used for riding therapy must be calm. Horses that become jumpy or excited by loud noises, sudden movements, or the sight of equipment such as wheelchairs and leg braces would not do well in riding therapy.

The age range for therapeutic horses is broad, as long as the horse is not too young or too old. The calmest horses are usually older and have spent a lot of time around people. A horse used for therapy is at least eight years old and some are as old as thirty.

Horses used in therapy must be well prepared. Proper training is important because their riders are special people. Therapy horses need to tolerate being bumped with crutches, canes, walkers, or wheelchairs.

For example, sometimes a child may remove his leg braces carelessly and toss them near the horse.

Mounting

Horses must be trained to stand still when being mounted in a variety of ways. Some students may use a **mounting block** to make them taller. Those in wheelchairs use a ramp. Their wheelchair is pushed up a ramp that makes the rider the same height as the saddle. Then they are lifted from the wheelchair to the saddle. Smaller riders are lifted from the mounting ramp onto the horse. Some riders are able to scramble onto the horse by themselves. Some, such as leg amputees, may only be able to mount on the right side. Thus, horses must learn to accept mounting from both sides, instead of only the traditional left-side mount.

A mounting block can help the rider mount the horse.

Some riders use a wheelchair ramp to mount the horse.

Calm Horses

Horses cannot become distracted during treatment sessions—even when games such as ball, ring, or bean-bag toss are being played. A therapy horse may have as many as four people walking around it at the same time. They include the leader (who holds the **lead line**), the instructor, and one or two volunteers, who are sidewalkers that keep the rider safe.

As therapists, horses help their patients' balance by stopping, starting, changing speed, and changing directions. As the horse moves, the rider is constantly thrown off balance. This requires the rider's muscles to contract and relax in attempting to rebalance. The instructor regulates these motions according to the rider's disability.

Horses must remain calm during sessions with the riders.

Sometimes children with disabilities kick, wiggle, bounce, and scream while on a horse. These riders have little control over their bodies or behavior and may easily slide off the horse's back. Instructors must make sure the horse can remain quiet for these lively patients. Calmness is a big part of a therapy horse's work and is part of its earliest training.

Twins Robert and Paul have autism, a developmental disability that is either present at birth or becomes evident during the first thirty months of life. As children, autistic individuals appear to be physically well developed. However, they are severely impaired in their ability to comprehend and communicate. Children or adults with autism may exhibit repeated body movements such as hand flapping and rocking, show unusual responses to people or objects, and resist changes in routine. In some cases, they may be aggressive.

By age two, Robert and Paul showed signs of autism. They did not look at people, did not speak, and did not respond to family members. They seemed to live in a dream world.

But horseback riding therapy changed all that. When they began therapy at age three, neither boy talked. Their parents communicated with them through sign language. Adding riding therapy to their clinical therapy had a dramatic effect on the twins. They began emerging from their isolation. Both boys began talking and reacting positively to people. Their mother is finding great hope for her sons through **equestrian** therapy. She affirms, "It's fun for the kids. It's therapy in disguise."[3]

Training

Instructors train the horses used in therapy. But instructors also need to go to school themselves. For example, Alexandra, a lifelong rider and a college graduate with a degree in physical education, decided to become an instructor at a riding center for the disabled. She completed a difficult three-month training program at Cheff Therapeutic Riding Center in Augusta, Michigan.

At Cheff Center, students are taught routine horse care and stable management. They learn human **anatomy**, **orthopedics**, physical therapy, and study the various disabilities that they are likely to encounter. After passing the course, Alexandra accepted a job at a residential school for retarded children. One of the most important parts of Alexandra's job is training horses for therapy work.

A new horse offered to the school must go through a three-month trial period before it is accepted. However, some trainers know within a week if the new horse has what it takes to be used with riders with disabilities. Many horses turn out to be unsuitable for use in therapeutic riding.

In general, horses that are not accepted are unsound, unhealthy, have back problems, or show signs of past abuse. Some may not be able to **trot** or **canter** easily because of a physical impairment. They may have arthritis or hoof and leg problems, conditions that would make the horse expensive to maintain. If the horse bites, nips, or shows aggressiveness, it will

All horses must pass training and a three-month trial period before being used in therapeutic riding.

Horses in training are rewarded with food and affection.

not be dependable. The horse needs to trust people or it cannot do its job.

Instructors must expose the horse to many situations to make sure it can handle the job. For example, instructor Alexandra subjected Sarah, a new horse, to the kinds of unusual treatment that she might get from the children. Alexandra flapped the **reins**, kicked Sarah in the ribs, and shrieked. She wiggled around in the saddle, bounced, or just went limp.

Next Alexandra asked another instructor to throw a ball in front of Sarah to see what the horse would do. Sarah jerked her head back out of the path of the ball, but she did not jump or bolt.

Alexandra rewarded Sarah with loving pats, praises, and apple or carrot treats when she did not flinch at these irritations. Soon Sarah learned to accept erratic behavior. Once a therapy horse has passed its training period, it is ready to perform its duties as a therapist. The horse becomes an important part of a team to treat the disabled.

Chapter Two

Therapy on Horseback

There are three types of therapeutic horseback riding: riding astride, **vaulting**, and **hippotherapy**. All three work primarily on physical disabilities.

Riding Astride

Riding astride (one leg on each side of the horse) uses an English saddle, a Western saddle, or a natural-ride saddle, which is made of soft felt secured with a handled strap. In riding astride classes, disabled riders learn to make the horse walk, trot, and do other skills with the help of a full team of instructors and sidewalkers. Some riders advance all the way up to independent riding. In some cases, riders will learn horse-grooming skills and even the names of the horse's riding equipment.

In riding astride, each rider always wears a safety helmet. The inexperienced rider has a horse leader and one or two sidewalkers. An independent rider will not have a leader but may have a sidewalker with an instructor giving directions. No rider is ever tied onto a horse, no matter how disabled. Instead someone will sit behind the rider, if needed.

First, the riders learn how to balance themselves. To practice balance, the riders hold their arms out at shoulder height as the horse is walked. To develop hand-eye

A safety helmet must be worn by all riders.

coordination and for fun, riders toss beanbags into spare tires, or loop rings over tall stakes set around the arena.

The next step is to have the instructor lead the horse over or around obstacles such as logs or poles. This improves the rider's balance and coordination further. It also helps muscles to become stronger and may lead to the rider being able to stand alone or even walk after riding for a period of time.

Improving balance in the saddle also adjusts the balancing part of the rider's inner ears. Sometimes this inner ear balance has never been developed because the disabled person may have been sitting in a wheelchair all of his or her life.

Ryan's Sessions

Ryan is a teenager with several disabilities. Because he cannot talk, he conveys messages with a communication board attached to his wheelchair. Ryan is in his sixth year of horse therapy. When Ryan first started in the program, he was very apprehensive. He fussed a lot and often hit himself in the chest out of protest or frustration.

Now he enjoys his biweekly sessions. When Ryan is lifted onto the horse, his arm and leg muscles are tight and stiff. His horse, named Starbaby, wears a special saddle that has Velcro strips attached to it. Ryan's jeans have Velcro sewn on the inner legs. The Velcro keeps Ryan from slipping out of position on the horse.

Ryan begins riding lying on his back to loosen up his muscles. Next his arms are raised and the muscles

Ryan is a therapeutic rider who communicates with a special board attached to his wheelchair.

begin to relax. Within fifteen minutes, Ryan's muscles have loosened enough for him to sit upright in the saddle with support from two sidewalkers. Later in the session, Ryan trots and laughs out loud with joy. Ryan's father is one of Ryan's volunteer sidewalkers and shares in his son's happiness on the horse.

Vaulting

Another type of therapeutic horseback riding is vaulting. Any person who has physical or emotional disabilities can receive the same benefits as from the riding astride program.

Vaulting is performing a variety of exercises on a moving horse's back. Using their arms and legs for support, the vaulters strengthen their muscles. They stand, kneel, sit, and lie down on the horse. These feats are performed on the horse's neck, back, and rump. The riders may face the horse's head, tail, or sides.

Most vaulters with disabilities are lifted onto the horse's back. Instead of a saddle for the rider to sit on, a thick pad covers the horse's back. The pad is secured by a leather surcingle, which is a band about six inches wide, that passes under the horse's belly. The surcingle has two handles on top, like those used by circus acrobatic riders.

Besides helping with physical disabilities, horses also help children who have emotional problems. An

Riders hold onto leather surcingles in vaulting exercises.

example of this takes place at a ranch where a group of thirty children, ages eight to twelve, arrive on a school bus. The children reside in a home for emotionally disturbed children. These children have been abused, neglected, and abandoned. Coming to the ranch and working with the horses on a steady basis helps them in many ways. The director explains:

> The animals capture and hold the children's interest which in itself is therapeutic. These youngsters have a short attention span, and they're usually unable to concentrate. Also, mastering their initial fear of such a large animal helps develop their self-esteem. They develop memory and self-control. To children who are accustomed to failing at virtually everything, all this is important.[4]

Most of the children excitedly head directly for the horse stalls. The instructors watch while they groom the animals with **currycombs** and brushes. Their next job is to put saddles and **bridles** on the horses. Everyone in the group shares in caring for the horses. They learn to lead and to groom, and learn the **tack** and safety rules.

After the kids finish in the stalls, they take turns performing vaulting exercises on a horse that wears a pad and vaulting surcingle. Each child, one at a time, runs to the horse and is boosted aboard. The exercises include standing up on the horse's back, standing on one foot, turning around completely, and lying on the horse's back. The children's faces radiate smiles of pride. For the emotionally disturbed children, a big plus of vaulting is trusting and working with others.

Riders learn to stand on their horses during a vaulting exercise.

Hippotherapy

A third form of horse therapy is hippotherapy. This is a combination of riding astride and vaulting, and is primarily for severe disability cases. "Hippo" means horse in Greek and applies to either speech, occupational, or physical therapy on horseback. In hippotherapy, the horse influences the patient rather than the patient influencing the horse. For example, Bryan, who is severely retarded, cannot sit or hold his head up without support. During his specialized therapy, he lies across the saddle on his belly. A therapist rides with Bryan to support his head and limbs and an instructor leads the horse around a ring at a slow walk.

The therapist and instructor are not sure how much Bryan absorbs during the experience. They believe that

Bryan is aware of the sounds, the smells, the warmth, and the motion of the horse. They know that the horse's movements give him exercise.

When Bryan tries to hold his head up, his neck muscles get stronger. The therapist hopes that Bryan's neck muscles will eventually grow strong enough for him to be held upright in the saddle.

Chapter Three

Blue Ribbon Events

The idea of handicapped competition on horses spread after the 1952 Olympics in Helsinki, Finland. At that event, Liz Hartel, a woman crippled from polio and confined to a wheelchair, won a silver medal in grand prix **dressage**. In grand prix dressage, a rider guides a horse through a series of difficult turns by slight movements of the hands, legs, and body.

Hartel's performance was a breakthrough achievement. Even though she had **polio**, the determined Danish horsewoman was not about to give up her riding. It encouraged other people with disabilities to also want to ride horses. Hartel's success inspired a formal movement in England promoting riding for the handicapped.

By 1969 the program had reached the United States and Canada. An organization called North American Riding for the Handicapped Association (NARHA) was formed. It promotes and supports therapeutic horseback riding.

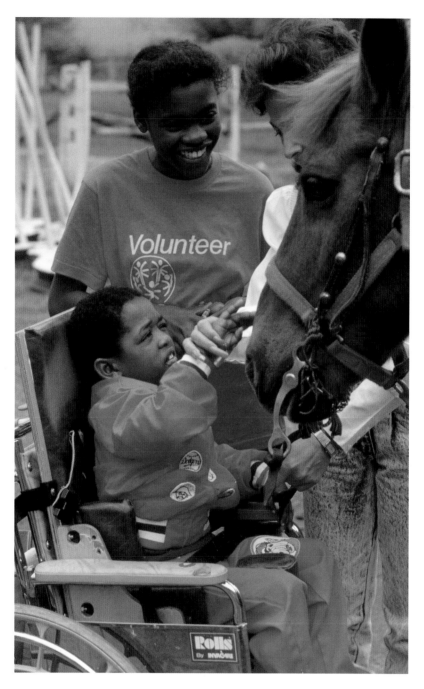

Therapeutic riding is considered one of the best methods for helping the disabled.

Today NARHA has over six hundred centers with four thousand therapy horses. Horseback riding is now considered one of the most effective and progressive methods of rehabilitation for the disabled.

Champion Competitors

The story of Mikko, age twenty-six, whose legs are **paralyzed** and whose eyesight is almost gone, gives hope to many others. Mikko, too, trained to be a competitor.

At age seventeen, Mikko was diagnosed with multiple sclerosis (MS), a prolonged disease of the central nervous system. MS follows a course of repeated **remissions** and worsening over a period of years. Gradually Mikko became completely paralyzed in the lower half of her body. She wanted to die.

But Mikko's mother restored Mikko's will to live when she told her about Therapeutic Equestrians, a horseback riding group for the disabled. When Mikko rode on a horse, she felt refreshed and energized. She credits riding with helping her survive. Mikko trained diligently for state, national, and international competitions. At the 1984 International Games for the Disabled, she won gold and silver medals. Mikko said, "I wanted to be a champion. Riding is vital to my life. I want to teach other people with [disabilities] not to give up."[5]

Each year several horse shows, exhibits, and play days are held for disabled riders. CALNET (California Network for Equestrian Therapy, Unlimited) State Championships is one of the largest horse shows for riders with mental and physical disabilities. At the 1999 event, 120 disabled riders from seventeen therapeutic riding centers in five states participated.

One person who has participated in many CALNET events is Vickie, who was born with Down's syndrome. Vickie's mother, Connie, describes how horse therapy changed her life:

Disabled riders often compete on horseback and win medals.

Vickie developed self-confidence through her relationship with the horse Mocha.

At age ten, Vickie met a big bay horse named Mocha. She learned how to groom and tack-up Mocha before each ride. He was so big and yet so very gentle with Vickie. Through the [building of] skills and friendship with Mocha, Vickie gained self-confidence. Through Vickie's new abilities, she entered horse shows for special equestrians. She participated in horse shows sponsored by Special Olympics and CAL-NET. Before each event she would be very nervous. But once she entered the arena on horseback, her self-assurance took over and she was in control of herself and her horse. Her trophy case proudly displays a total of fifteen blue ribbons and numerous trophies.[6]

Paul, a thirteen-year-old with Down's syndrome, participated in horseback riding therapy for three years before he was brave enough to enter the Special Olympics. He memorized ten steering commands for guiding his horse through the obstacle course of fences and barrels. On the day of the event, Paul won a **blue ribbon**.

A horse helped him gain the confidence and courage to do something he could not do three years earlier. Paul had progressed from lying flat against the horse's neck while clinging to its mane, to sitting tall in the saddle and learning commands, to becoming a winner.

Competitive Events

Some centers have Fun Days or Play Days where disabled children compete in a variety of different activities including pole bending. Pole bending is a timed event where the rider weaves between six upright poles set in a straight line twenty-one feet apart. Riding patterns in the race include all walking, all trotting, all cantering, or a combination of the three.

Another competitive event is equitation. Equitation is the art and knowledge of riding a horse. Riders are judged by their posture and ability to control the horse.

It requires a great deal of practice for the rider to learn balance and rhythm. In competition, equitation classes are in an arena and judged at various levels depending on the rider's ability. With the rider and horse working as one, the rider can walk only; or walk and trot; or walk, trot, and canter.

Families and friends are invited to attend these events, which include food, auctions, and other activities. An example of a Play Day game is Bucket Brigade, which is a team relay race. Competitors ride their horses to the end of the arena to get a cup of water. They carry the cup of water to their team's bucket in the middle of the arena, pouring it into the bucket. They ride back to their next team member to hand off the empty cup. The team with the most water in its bucket

Riders compete in activities such as pole bending on Fun Days.

Riders compete in a vaulting event.

at the end is the winner. Participants ride horses with a horse leader and sidewalkers as needed. All events are for pleasure and all competitors receive ribbons, medals, or certificates.

There are also competitions for vaulters. Vaulting activities are performed as singles, doubles, and sometimes in combination with people who are nondisabled. There are seven compulsory, or required, exercises that vaulters must learn if they want to enter competitions, which are open to everyone. The maneuvers include the vault-on or mount, basic seat, flag, mill, scissors, stand, and flank or dismount, performed in that order. During the exercises, the horse moves in a wide circle around the inner edge of the ring.

In the basic seat, a vaulter sits erect on the horse and holds on to both handles. The vaulter lets go of both

Vaulting can be done by two riders together.

handles at the same time and stretches arms straight out for a count of four.

In executing the flag, the vaulter starts from the sitting position, then kneels. The right leg stretches straight back while the left arm reaches straight up and forward. The arm, back, and leg form an arc. The body is supported with the right hand on the surcingle handle and the left knee on the horse's back.

The mill is the third required exercise. Sitting on the horse, a vaulter turns a complete circle by alternately moving legs and hands in four turns.

The scissors is the most difficult exercise. From a sitting position, the vaulter holds on to the handles of the surcingle, then swings the legs forward and backward. While the legs are over the horse's rump, the

Two children perform the longbridge vaulting exercise.

gait: Any of the ways a horse can move by lifting its feet in a certain rhythm.

hippotherapy: A combination of riding astride and vaulting that is used primarily with the severely disabled.

lead line: A rope attached to the halter used to lead or guide a horse.

mental retardation: A brain impairment which slows learning.

mounting block: A block used by riders to stand on, making it easier to mount their horse.

multiple sclerosis: A disease of the central nervous system characterized by partial or complete paralysis and muscle tremors.

orthopedics: The branch of medicine that deals with disorders of the bones, joints, and associated muscles.

paralysis: Loss of the ability to feel sensation or to move a part of the body.

polio: An infectious disease that occurs mainly in children and, in its severe form, attacks the central nervous system and produces paralysis and muscle deterioration.

reins: Straps attached to the bit and held by the rider to control the horse's movements.

remission: A temporary lessening of a disease or pain.

spina bifida: A birth defect that creates a hole in the spinal column, which may lead to paralysis and brain damage.

tack: A horse's riding equipment.

therapist: A person (or animal) who applies treatment to cure or heal a disability.

trot: A two-beat diagonal gait. The horse's right front and left rear legs move in tandem, with the left front and right rear legs following.

vaulting: A form of horse therapy that uses gymnastic-type exercises.

walk: The slowest gait; a four-beat gait where each hoof touches the ground individually.

Notes

Introduction: The Horse's Natural Gift

1. Quoted in Andrew Jones, "A Boy Who Climbed the Marigold," *Reader's Digest*, February 1987, p. 98.
2. Quoted in Caren Marcus, "She Helps Disabled Kids Ride High," *Good Housekeeping*, October 1997, p. 23.

Chapter One: Horse Training

3. Quoted in Angela M. Lemire, "Horse Therapy," *Los Angeles Daily News*, October 17, 1999, p. 3.

Chapter Two: Therapy on Horseback

4. Quoted in Patricia Curtis, *Animal Partners*. New York: E. P. Dutton, 1982, pp. 22–23.

Chapter Three: Blue Ribbon Events

5. Quoted in Vernon Scott, "The Triumph of Mikko Mayeda," *Good Housekeeping*, March 1987, p. 40.
6. Interview with Connie M. Gilly, director, Special Equestrian Riding Therapy, Chatsworth, California, April 2000.

Glossary

anatomy: The position, structure, and arrangement of body parts.

autism: A brain disorder characterized by repetitive movements and by being unable to interact socially.

blue ribbon: The prize awarded to the first-place rider in a horse-show division.

bridle: A strap that slips over the horse's head. The bit and reins attach to it and it is used for riding.

canter: A gait slower than the gallop, but faster than the trot, in a three-beat rhythm.

cerebral palsy: Paralysis due to an injury of the brain usually suffered at birth and characterized by spasms.

currycomb: A handheld tool made of flexible rubber bumps to rub off caked dirt from the coat of a horse.

disability: An impairment or medical condition that prevents someone from performing a specific task or function.

Down's syndrome: A condition caused by irregular cells during the mother's pregnancy and characterized by mental retardation, unusual facial features, and sometimes poor hearing or vision.

dressage: A French word meaning "training"; progressing from basic to very complex levels of movements.

equestrian: Relating to horseback riding.

Therapeutic horseback riding helps many disabled children.

vaulter passes the left leg over the right leg and ends up sitting backward. With arms on the handles behind, the vaulter throws the left leg over right again to turn back in the same direction to a front sitting position.

To stand on the horse, a vaulter begins from a sitting position, places the weight on the arms and snaps both legs up to a kneeling position facing forward, then softly hops to the feet.

Noncompulsory exercises are called Kür, also known as freestyle competition. Vaulters sometimes perform Kür exercises to music. Examples include the candle (lying on the horse's back with legs straight up and perpendicular to the ground) and the longbridge (which two children do together). For example, in a recent competition, in performing the longbridge, a young boy was lifted onto the horse's padded back. The boy lay on his back with his head resting on the horse's rump. Next, a five-year-old girl with leg braces was lifted onto the horse. She faced the horse's head with her hands on the surcingle handles while the boy held up her legs. In this position, the girl balanced her body above the boy. The horse then slowly made its way around the ring with a safety walker on each side.

All Riders Are Winners

Whether riders compete or not, they are all winners in the sense that they are involved in a new adventure that increases strength, knowledge, and self-esteem.

For many disabled children, riding is the best thing that happens in their lives. It provides a sense of freedom and self-reliance and allows them to forget their problems, at least for a while. Their grinning faces tell the story. They are on a path to independent living. And it is all because of a horse.

Index

age, 9
Alexandra, 13–14, 15–16
autism, 6, 12

balance, 11–12, 18–19
Bryan, 23–24
Bucket Brigade, 31

calmness, 9, 11–12
CALNET (California Network for Equestrian Therapy Unlimited), 27–30
cerebral palsy, 5, 6–8
Cheff Therapeutic Riding Center, 13
competitions
    Fun Days, 30–31
    International Games for the Disabled, 27
    Olympics, 25
    Special Olympics, 29, 30
    for vaulters, 32–36
Connie, 28–30
coordination, 18–19

Down's syndrome, 6, 30
dressage, 25

emotionally disturbed children, 20–23
equestrian therapy. *See* horse therapy
equitation, 30–31

freestyle competitions, 35
Fun Days, 30–31

gait, 7, 14
grooming, 22

Hartel, Liz, 25
hippotherapy, 23
horse therapy, 12–13
    goals of, 4–5
    hippotherapy, 23
    riding astride, 17–19
    vaulting, 20–23

instructors, 13
International Games for the Disabled, 27

through education, communication, standards, and research for people with and without disabilities.

Ride on Therapeutic Horsemanship
Broken Tree Ranch
21126 Chatsworth Street
Chatsworth, CA 91311
(818) 700-2971
www.rideon.org
A therapeutic riding program for all those with disabilities and their families. Ride on is accredited and insured through the North American Riding for the Handicapped Association.

Special Equestrian Riding Therapy (SERT)
P.O. Box 1098
Agoura Hills, CA 91376-1098
(818) 776-6476
www.sert.org
The riding center is located at 9633 Baden Avenue in Chatsworth and is accredited and insured through the North American Riding for the Handicapped Association.

For Further Exploration

Barbara Adams, *Like It Is: Facts and Feelings About Handicaps from Kids Who Know.* New York: Walker, 1979. A group of youngsters discuss their disabilities and how they cope with them on a day-to-day basis.

Pete Sanders and Steve Myers, *People with Disabilities.* Brookfield, CT: Copper Beech Books, 1998. Describing many disabilities, this book tells how people can understand and change their attitudes and their children's attitudes toward people with disabilities.

Bernard Wolf, *Don't Feel Sorry for Paul.* New York: J. B. Lippincott, 1974. A photo essay of a seven-year-old boy with disabilities. The story shows how Paul has learned to live successfully in a world made for people without disabilities.

Organizations to Contact

The following organizations can supply information about people with disabilities and about horse therapy ranches. Contact them by mail, telephone, or through their website.

Ahead with Horses, Inc.
9311 Del Arroyo Drive
Sun Valley, CA 91352
(818) 767-6373
Provides therapy on horseback through vaulting.

American Vaulting Association National Office (AVA)
642 Alford Place
Bainbridge Island, WA 98110
(206) 780-9353
www.americanvaulting.org
The AVA promotes the sport of vaulting in the United States as a member of the American Horse Shows Association. It lists meetings, books, clubs, vaulting exhibitions, compulsories, and Kür competitions.

Cheff Therapeutic Riding Center
8450 North 43rd Street
Augusta, MI 49012
(616) 731-4471

www.cheffcenter.com
The world's largest school built exclusively to teach riding to the disabled.

Heads Up, Inc.
30757 Bouquet Canyon Road
Saugus, CA 91350
(661) 297-7433
Provides therapy on horseback for disabled and at-risk youths.

National Information Center for Children and Youth with Disabilities (NICHCY)
P.O. Box 1492
Washington, DC 20013-1492
(800) 695-0285
www.nichcy.org
NICHCY is the national information and referral center that provides information on disabilities and disability-related issues for families, educators, and other professionals. Their special focus is children and youth (to age twenty-two).

North American Riding for the Handicapped Association (NARHA)
P.O. Box 33150
Denver, CO 80233
(800) 369-7433
www.narha.org
NARHA is a membership organization that fosters safe, professional, ethical, and therapeutic equine activities

Picture Credits

About the Author

Judith Janda Presnall earned her bachelor's degree in education from the University of Wisconsin, Whitewater. She began her writing career in 1985, eventually focusing on nonfiction. Some of her books include *Life on Alcatraz, Mount Rushmore, Oprah Winfrey, The Giant Panda, Artificial Organs,* and *Rachel Carson.* Franklin Watts published *Circuses, Animal Skeletons,* and *Animals that Glow.* In addition to *Horse Therapists,* Presnall has also written *Police Dogs, Navy Dolphins, Guide Dogs,* and *Animal Actors* for KidHaven Press's Animals with Jobs series. Presnall lives in Los Angeles, California, with her husband, Lance, and three cats. They have two adult children, Kaye and Kory.